GUT-BUSTING
Puns
FOR
MINECRAFTERS

ENDERMEN, EXPLOSIONS, WITHERS, AND MORE!

Also by Brian Boone:

Hysterical Jokes for Minecrafters: Blocks, Boxes, Blasts, and Blow-Outs, Book 3

Side-Splitting Jokes for Minecrafters: Ghastly Golems and Ghoulish Ghasts, Book 4

Uproarious Riddles for Minecrafters: Mobs, Ghasts, Biomes, and More! Book 5

The Know-It-All Trivia Book for Minecrafters: Over 800 Amazing Facts and Insider Secrets

The Unofficial Harry Potter Joke Book: Great Guffaws for Gryffindor

GUT-BUSTING
Puns
FOR
MINECRAFTERS

ENDERMEN, EXPLOSIONS, WITHERS, AND MORE!

BRIAN BOONE

Illustrations by Amanda Brack

Sky Pony Press
New York

Copyright © 2018 by Hollan Publishing, Inc.

Minecraft® is a registered trademark of Notch Development AB.

The Minecraft game is copyright © Mojang AB.

Sky Pony Press books may be purchased in bulk at special discounts for sales promotion, corporate gifts, fund-raising, or educational purposes. Special editions can also be created to specifications. For details, contact the Special Sales Department, Sky Pony Press, 307 West 36th Street, 11th Floor, New York, NY 10018 or info@skyhorsepublishing.com.

Sky Pony® is a registered trademark of Skyhorse Publishing, Inc.®, a Delaware corporation.

Visit our website at www.skyponypress.com.

10 9 8 7 6 5 4 3 2 1

Library of Congress Cataloging-in-Publication Data is available on file.

Cover illustration by Amanda Brack
Cover design by Brian Peterson

Paperback ISBN: 978-1-5107-2718-2
Ebook ISBN: 978-1-5107-2723-6

Printed in Canada

CONTENTS

INTRODUCTION

D o you want to "build" up a supply of *Minecraft* jokes? Ready for a joke book about the best game in the world that really "rocks"? Want some jokes about Hostiles and Passives and tools and Steve that are so funny you'll "axe" for more? Well, then it's time to stop "tooling" around and make room in your chest for *Gut-Busting Puns for Minecrafters: Endermen, Explosions, Withers, and More*.

We don't "mine" telling you that it's most fantastic, pun-tasting book yet in our *Jokes for Minecrafters* series. And "wither" you like it or not, you're going to explode with laughter. Don't worry, it's not "The End"! We don't want to "Creeper" you out! We think you'll agree that it's just so much fun talking about *Minecraft,* especially in a way that can make you and your friends laugh . . . "ore" maybe drive them a little crazy with some real groaners. Inside you'll find all kinds of wordplay, word jokes, silly fun, and silly puns all about your favorite game: *Minecraft*!

CHAPTER 1

A MOB OF HOSTILE MOB JOKES

Q: What do you get when you cross a Blaze with a mineshaft?

A: Fire in the hole!

■

Q: What did the hip Blaze say when it discovered *Minecraft*?

A: "This is fire!"

■

Q: What happens when a Ghast gets lost in the fog?

A: It's mist.

Q: What do you call a Zombie Pigman with three eyes?

A: A Zombie Piiigman.

Q: How does a Creeper listen to music?

A: With a boombox.

Q: What do you get when you cross a Creeper with a Sheep?

A: A Sheep that creeps.

Q: Where did the Zombie Pigman go when it died?
A: Hog Heaven.

■

Q: What happened to Steve when he met a Creeper on a blustery day?
A: First he got blown up . . . and then he got blown away.

■

Q: What will you never get from a Creeper?
A: First-hand information or second-hand news.

■

Q: What's a Blaze's favorite day?
A: Ash Wednesday.

■

Q: How can you tell when someone has met a Blaze?
A: They look ashen.

■

Q: What steps should you take if a Blaze is about to attack?
A: Long ones!

Q: Why couldn't the Creeper feel his legs?

A: Because it didn't have any arms.

■

Q: Why are Ghasts white and blocky?

A: Because it they were white and round they wouldn't be in *Minecraft*!

■

Q: How do you know a creeper has been visiting your house?

A: Because you came back and your house had been blown up.

■

Q: Why are the Creepers green?

A: They must be jealous.

■

Q: How do zombies get so good at *Minecraft*?

A: Dead-ication.

Q: What do Creepers put on their ice cream?
A: Whipped scream.

∎

Q: What's a Skeleton's favorite rock band?
A: The Grateful Dead.

∎

Q: What did the Zombie say to the Villager?
A: "Nice to eat you!"

∎

Q: What do Australian Creepers use to hunt?
A: BOOM-a-rangs.

∎

Q: What kind of house do Creepers live in?
A: Greenhouses.

∎

Q: What does a backward Creeper do?
A: Puts itself back together.

Q: What do you call a Skeleton that won't wake up?
A: Bone tired!

■

Q: Why couldn't the Creeper reach the top shelf?
A: He needed a hand.

■

Q: What did the Creeper get on his test?
A: Creeper bits.

■

Q: Why did the Spider Jockey cross the road?
A: Because it was riding a Spider that was crossing the road!

■

Q: What should you give a Creeper?
A: Plenty of room!

■

Q: How do Mobs say goodbye?
A: "Hostile mañana!"

Q: What kind of underwear do Creepers wear?

A: Fruit of the Boom.

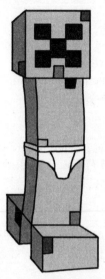

Q: What do Creepers use to build things?

A: Concreep.

Q: Where should you avoid if you don't want to run into Zombies?

A: Dead ends.

Q: Where do Creepers stay when they're traveling through Europe?

A: In Hostiles.

■

Q: Why did Steve avoid the daytime Zombie?

A: Because he was shade-y.

■

Q: If you're worried about exploding Creepers, what's the best thing that can happen?

A: The Creeper explodes. Then you don't have to worry anymore!

■

Q: What burns but doesn't explode?

A: A Creeper on top of a block.

■

Q: What's the creepiest Mob in *Minecraft*?

A: Creepers!

Q: What happened when Steve threw some cobwebs at a Spider?

A: Nothing!

■

Q: Why don't Zombies smell?

A: Because they're dead and their noses don't work!

■

Q: What do you get when you cross a Ghast and an Ocelot?

A: A scaredy cat!

■

Q: Why was the Zombie grouchy?

A: It wasn't a mourning person.

■

Q: What has six feet and can spell very well?

A: A of Witches.

Q: Why do Ghasts like mine elevators?
A: It raises their spirits.

■

Q: Why did the Ghast explode?
A: He was wondering what it would be like to be a Creeper.

■

Q: Why are Creepers green?
A: So they can hide in the grass!

■

Q: What's green and has four legs?
A: Two Creepers.

■

Q: What happens when you cross a Tree with some Witches?
A: A Tree-o.

■

Q: What's black, white, and explodes?
A: A Creeper on a black-and-white monitor.

Q: What contract do Mobs agree to?
A: The Magma Carta.

■

Q: What room does a Zombie not need?
A: The living room.

■

Q: What does a Magma Cube take for a headache?
A: Ashpirin.

■

Q: Why was the Blaze a terrible boss?
A: It was always firing everyone.

■

Q: Why shouldn't you ever go to a Ghast's house?
A: It's Nether home.

■

Q: How many Zombies do you need to change a Torch?
A: None. They like it dark anyway.

Q: Why did the Spider spin webs?

A: It didn't know how to knit.

■

Q: Why do Ghasts shoot fireballs?

A: Because if they shot waterballs, they would evaporate.

■

Q: What do you call a Skeleton that won't attack?

A: Lazy bones.

■

Q: Why are Creepers like bubble gum?

A: They both blow up!

■

Q: How do you kill a Creeper without risking damage?

A: Give it a mirror!

■

Q: What do you get if you put a saddle on a Zombie Pigman?

A: A road hog.

Q: Why did Steve have to abandon his house?
A: Too many skeletons in his closet.

Q: Where do Creepers keep their money?
A: In a Creepurse.

Q: What would you call a Zombie Pigman that knows karate?
A: A pork chop.

Q: Why was the Ghast so sad?
A: Oh, Nether mind.

■

Q: What happened to the Creeper who became a really big star?
A: He blew up!

■

Q: How do know if there will be a three-headed monster in your area?
A: Just check the Wither report.

■

Q: Why do Cave Spiders live in caves?
A: Because real estate prices are so high.

■

Q: How does Steve avoid a fight with a Hostile Mob?
A: He mines his own business.

■

Q: Why did the police arrest a Hostile?
A: They caught it Creeping around.

Q: Why does Slime in *Minecraft* fly?
A: Because Slime flies when you're having fun!

■

Q: How do Slime move around?
A: With a Slime Machine.

■

Q: Where's the best place to learn about Slime?
A: Goo-gle.

■

Q: What do you call a little Slime?
A: Slim.

■

Q: What was Steve doing near a mob spawner?
A: Creeping warm.

■

Q: Who's the most educated Mob in *Minecraft*?
A: The Magma Cube—it has so many degrees.

Q: Why doesn't anyone want to play with a Vex?
A: It's for the birds!

■

Q: Why are there no bugs in *Minecraft*?
A: Probably because the Spiders ate them all!

■

Q: What room do Creepers feel most comfortable in?
A: The Boom-Boom Room.

■

Q: On what day are you most likely to see Strays?
A: Stray Day.

■

Q: What flowers do Skeletons like best?
A: Yarrows.

■

Q: Where do Zombie Pigmen sleep?
A: In their hammocks.

Q: Why did the skeleton shoot at Steve's lower legs for a change?

A: It was all a bunch of below-knee.

■

Q: What do you call a fake Mob?

A: An Hostile impasta.

■

Q: How did Steve get blown up doing yard work?

A: He was trimming what he thought was a hedge . . . but it was a Creeper.

■

Q: Why couldn't the skeleton fall in love?

A: He didn't have the heart.

■

Q: Which is the smartest Hostile Mob?

A: The Wither, because three heads are better than one.

Q: What would happen if there had been creepers in 1800s Europe?

A: Napoleon Blown-Apart!

■

Q: How do you make a Witch itch?

A: Take away the "W."

■

Q: Can you get fur from a Killer Bunny?

A: Yes, as fur away as possible!

■

Q: What do you get when you cross a Creeper and a cat?

A: A Creepurrrrrrr.

Q: What's the most dangerous thing to find in a *Minecraft* Tree?

A: A Creeper that learned to climb Trees.

■

Q: Where do you always find a Ghast?

A: The Ghast place you look!

■

Q: Witch Mob makes potions?

A: Exactly!

■

Q: How would you greet a Wither?

A: "Hello, hello, hello!"

■

Q: Who's the Creeper who created *Minecraft*?

A: Markussssss Perssssssssson.

■

Q: Why aren't Zombie Pigmen very grateful?

A: They take everything for grunted.

Q: What kind of SUV does a Hostile drive?

A: A Creep!

■

Q: What burns in the daytime . . . unless it's in the shade?

A: A Zombie.

■

Q: What did the Guardian get on its report card?

A: All Seas.

■

Q: There are no insects in *Minecraft*, but there are flies. How?

A: The Vex flies!

CHAPTER 2

ROCKS AND BLOCKS

Q: Where do Minecrafters buy their clothes?
A: Off the Netherrack.

■

Q: What happens to stone, rocks, and Ore when they get broken up?
A: They un-gravel!

■

Q: How did they catch the Redstone thief?
A: Red-handed!

■

Q: What kind of dirt gets stuck in Steve's shoes the most?
A: Sole sand.

Q: Why did Steve put Wood planks on his bed?

A: He wanted to sleep like a log.

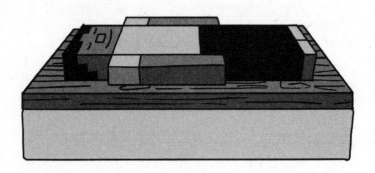

Q: Who's the president of *Minecraft*?

A: A Rock Obama.

■

Q: What's the difference between Gravel and a more valuable Ore?

A: One is coarse, and the other is quartz.

■

Q: What's the deadliest gem?

A: Die-mond.

Q: **What are Steve's favorite kind of ores?**
A: Met-Alex.

■

Q: **If H2O is the formula for water, then what's the formula for ice?**
A: H2O cubed.

■

Q: **Where does a *Minecrafter* like to relax?**
A: In a rocking chair.

■

Q: **Where would you find sleeping ore?**
A: In the bedrock.

■

Q: **What kind of ore shows up on St. Patrick's Day?**
A: Sham rock.

■

Q: **How do you make Stone float?**
A: Put it in a glass with some ice cream and root beer.

Q: What did Steve have for lunch when he went to a Japanese restaurant?

A: A Bento box.

Q: How does Steve secure his bike?

A: He blocks it up.

■

Q: What happened when Steve discovered a lode of Obsidian?

A: Everything went black!

■

Q: Why is it kind of bad to discover Obsidian?

A: It's really tough!

Q: What happened when water met lava?
A: They made Obsidian!

■

Q: Why is Sandstone such a good friend?
A: It's very supportive.

■

Q: How does Sandstone answer the phone?
A: "Yellow!"

■

Q: Where would you go without Bedrock?
A: Everywhere and nowhere all at once.

■

Q: What does cobblestone leave behind when it's mined?
A: Holes!

■

Q: What sign would work on Podzol?
A: "Keep off the grass!"

Q: **Why was Steve shy?**
A: Because he was the new kid on the block.

■

Q: **What do Blazes use to build things?**
A: Cinder blocks.

■

Q: **What was young Steve's favorite toy?**
A: His Jack-in-the-Box.

■

Q: **Why did Steve place Wood Stairs near Brick stairs?**
A: He wanted to have a stairing contest.

■

Q: **Why do Glowstones do well in school?**
A: They're very bright.

■

Q: **Where does a Minecrafter keep all their tips and
    strategies?**
A: In a Note Block.

Q: Why did Notch make such a good game?

A: Because he thought *inside* the box.

∎

Q: Why did the Minecrafter tear down his building and start again?

A: He didn't want to get boxed in.

∎

Q: What do you call a Cobblestone thief?

A: A Cobble-robber.

Q: What would you be if you had a billion air blocks?
A: A billion-air!

■

Q: How did Steve feel after covering his house in gold?
A: Gilty.

■

Q: What did Alex say to Steve when she discovered a ton of emeralds?
A: "Get a lode of this!"

■

Q: How is milk sold in *Minecraft*?
A: By the quartz.

■

Q: Why didn't the Minecrafter do anything when he came across a ton of stone?
A: He wanted a clean slate.

Q: Why don't miners mess much with the remains of old buildings?

A: They're nothing but rubble!

■

Q: Why was the miner upset?

A: His job was in ruins!

■

Q: What has legs but can't walk?

A: A miner's Work Bench.

■

Q: What happened when the builder didn't have enough supports?

A: He was on the brick of disaster.

■

Q: What magical substance is *Minecraft* made of?

A: Pixel Dust.

Q: What happens when you talk to a Minecrafter while they're playing?

A: You'll get a stony silence.

■

Q: Where do Minecrafters go to college?

A: Prince-stone.

■

Q: Where do Minecrafters get gas?

A: The Chevrock station.

■

Q: What music do Minecrafters prefer?

A: Rock!

■

Q: Why should you play *Minecraft*?

A: Ore else!

■

Q: How do you get good luck in *Minecraft*?

A: Knock on Wood!

Q: Why do woodpeckers love to play *Minecraft*?
A: Because of all the Wood!

■

Q: What toy do '80s Minecraters love?
A: The Rubik's Cube.

■

Q: What kind of office setup would Minecrafters enjoy?
A: Cubicles.

■

Q: Why didn't Notch use spheres to make *Minecraft*?
A: Because cubes had the edge!

■

Q: What kind of art do Minecrafters like best?
A: Cubism.

■

Q: Where do Minecrafters invest their treasure?
A: In the block market.

Q: What's the Minecrafter's dream sportscar?

A: The Porsche Boxster.

■

Q: What kind of old-fashioned dances do Steve and Alex go to?

A: Box socials.

■

Q: Why do Minecrafters play while sitting in gaming chairs?

A: Because they rock!

■

Q: What instrument does Steve play?

A: The blockenspiel.

■

Q: What do Minecrafters call television?

A: The idiot box.

Q: **What happened when Steve planted some flowers next to some TNT blocks?**

A: They went ka-BLOOM!

■

Q: **What creature haunts *Minecraft* . . . but has never been verified?**

A: The Block Ness Monster.

■

Q: **How did Steve make sure nobody stole his Redstone?**

A: He used his block-locks.

■

Q: **Why don't Minecrafters mind being on Santa's naughty list?**

A: Because they'd *love* to get Coal!

■

Q: **What Block never sticks around for long?**

A: Leaves.

Q: How did Steve make his table bigger when he was all out of Wood?

A: He put a leaf in it!

■

Q: How did Steve tell Alex he was going out to mine?

A: He left a Note Block.

■

Q: Why did the lawyer enjoy *Minecraft*?

A: Because he could build his own Quartz-room!

■

Q: What happened when a player took all the TNT they could find and put it next to a single block of Bedrock?

A: Nothing!

■

Q: Why couldn't Steve ever build a Portal?

A: He Nether had enough Obsidian!

Q: Why did the player collect so many Beacons?
A: They were just calling out to him.

■

Q: Why did the Noob make a house out of Sponge Blocks?
A: She wanted to soak everything in!

■

Q: What did the Minecrafter say when they hit a lode of Lapis Lazuli ore?
A: "How enchanting!"

■

Q: What kind of Wood would you find in watery biomes?
A: Plank-ton.

■

Q: What *Minecraft* flower is made of stone?
A: Ore-chids.

■

Q: Why did the player fill their shelter with Wood planks?
A: To "spruce" it up!

Q: **What's the least stable building block?**
A: Hobblestone.

◼

Q: **How did the Minecrafter know what would happen in her game?**
A: She found a Crystal Block.

◼

Q: **What outdoor game would a Minecrafter never do?**
A: Skip stones!

◼

Q: **When is a liquid a solid, and a solid a liquid?**
A: When it's a Water Block.

◼

Q: **What do you call a *Minecraft* clock that goes up to 13?**
A: Broken!

◼

Q: **What gem starts with M?**
A: An *Em*erald.

Q: Why did Steve take some of Alex's wood?
A: He wanted to play a plank on her.

■

Q: How did Steve like the trees in the Forest?
A: He thought they were oak-ay.

■

Q: What's TNT's favorite holiday?
A: New Year's Eve—it loves the countdown!

■

Q: What's a better name for a block of Ice?
A: A brrr-ick.

■

Q: Why do Minecrafters chase leprechauns?
A: They're looking for the pot of gold!

■

Alex: Why are you carrying two Blocks when I'm carrying four?

Steve: I guess you're just too lazy to make two trips!

Q: Why did the Minecrafter always keep a deck of cards by his computer?

A: In case he needed Diamonds.

Q: What do Minecrafters wear to bed?

A: Gemmies.

Q: Poor Steve had a cold.

A: His nose was completely blocked.

Q: How is *Minecraft* like a concert?

A: It's full of rock stars!

■

Q: How many blocks can you fit inside an empty Chest?

A: Just one, because after the first one it's no longer empty!

■

Q: How do you make others change direction in *Minecraft*?

A: You block their path!

■

Q: Why hasn't *Minecraft 2* come out?

A: Notch has Coder's Block!

CHAPTER 3

DID YOU HEAR . . . ?

Q: Did you hear the joke about The End?

A: Never mind, It's over your head.

■

Q: Did you hear the joke about the Ice Mountains?

A: Never mind, it's just a big bluff.

■

Q: Did you hear about Minecraft Airlines?

A: All the flights are square trip.

■

Q: Did you hear about the player who forgot to save his game?

A: It was an Axe-ident.

Q: Did you hear about the Creeper?

A: He really lost his head!

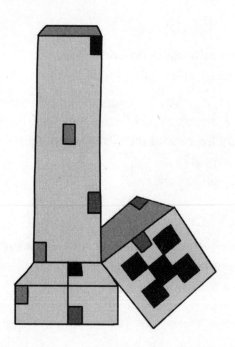

Q: Did you hear about the rocks that ran away from the mineshaft?

A: They were tired of being taken for granite.

Q: Did you hear about the grumpy Creeper?

A: It threw a hissssssssy fit.

■

Q: Did you hear about the ore?

A: It got smashed into total Obsidian.

■

Q: Did you hear about the Silverfish who discovered a trove of gold?

A: It's a Goldfish now.

■

Q: Did you hear about the Minecrafter's beautiful diamond tower?

A: It was a real gem!

■

Q: Did you hear Steve got sick from mining too much?

A: His voice was all gravelly.

Q: Did you hear about the miner who died in the Nether?

A: Apparently, he fell head over heels in lava.

■

Q: Did you hear there weren't many Hostile Mobs out the other night?

A: It was a real Skeleton Crew.

■

Q: Did you hear Notch didn't want to include shears?

A: They were almost cut!

■

Q: Did you see how Steve fought off that Zombie Pigman horde?

A: It was oink-credible!

■

Q: Did you hear about the time-traveling Hostile?

A: It was a real Ghast from the past.

Q: Did you hear that *Minecraft* went on sale?

A: It was a square deal.

■

Q: Did you hear about the Hostile who wrote its memoirs?

A: It used a Ghast-writer.

■

Q: Did you hear about the Cart that didn't work?

A: It was a Brokeswagon.

■

Q: Did you hear about the embarrassingly massive lode of ore?

A: It was obsidian!

■

Q: Did you hear about the Sheep that didn't want to come near Steve?

A: It was baaaa-shful.

Q: Did you hear about the Zombie Pigman who was a show-off?

A: What a ham!

■

Q: Did you hear about the injured Zombie Pigman?

A: He had to be taken away in a hambulance.

■

Q: Did you hear about the latest Witches' potion?

A: It blew everybody away.

■

Q: Did you hear about the tree that Steve punched?

A: First it had leaves, and then it had to leave.

■

Q: Did you hear Steve forgot the only way to get Netherrack was with a Pickaxe?

A: It's true, he Netherracked his brain . . . and still couldn't think of it.

Q: Did you hear about the *Minecraft* movie?
A: It was da bomb!

■

Q: Did you hear about the huge mobs of Shulkers?
A: It was intensity in End cities!

■

Q: Did you hear about the confident Shulker?
A: It finally came out of its shell.

■

Q: Did you hear about the lazy Shulker?
A: It was a shell of its former self.

■

Q: Did you hear about how Alex avoided the angry Guardian?
A: The laser didn't phase her!

■

Q: Did you hear about the Guardian who couldn't stop shooting laser beams?
A: It was just going through a phase.

Q: Did you hear about the Guardian's new spikes?

A: It really extended itself!

Q: Did you hear about the aggressive Evoker?

A: It really went for the jugular!

■

Q: Did you hear about the lazy End City hostile?

A: He really Shulked his duties.

Q: Did you hear about the claustrophobic *Minecrafter*?

A: He felt boxed in.

Q: Did you hear about the Evoker attacking Steve?

A: He thought it was fangtastic!

Q: Did you hear about the Evoker who went fishing?

A: He got lots of bites!

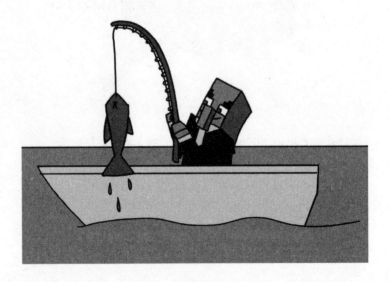

Q: Did you hear about the Skeleton that got caught in the rain?

A: It made a rain-bow.

■

Q: Did you hear about the Zombie Pigman that got too close to the Evoker?

A: It ended in smoked ham.

■

Q: Did you hear about the Guardian who shot beams while it was asleep?

A: He was having a laser kind of day.

■

Q: Did you hear that Steve used to date a Hostile?

A: Now she's his ex-Vex-girlfriend.

■

Q: Did you hear about the mob of Guardians?

A: It was monumental!

Q: Did you hear about the Guardian they put on trial for blasting players with a laser?

A: It was found gill-ty.

■

Q: Did you hear about the Witch in the chilly biome?

A: She was having a cold spell.

Q: Did you hear about the Blaze?

A: It got elected to the Hall of Flame.

■

Q: Did you hear that all Steve's friends bought him an Axe?

A: Yep, they all chipped in.

■

Q: Did you hear what happened to Steve when he was putting up a roof?

A: He got shingles.

■

Q: Did you hear about the Wolf who wandered into the Desert biome?

A: He was a hot dog.

■

Q: Did you hear about the Creeper that got a job as a librarian?

A: It was very good at telling people "ssssh!"

Q: Did you hear about Steve's adventure in the Extreme Hills?

A: It was a real cliffhanger!

■

Q: Did you hear about the builder who filled his house with Activators and Detectors?

A: He really went off the rails.

■

Q: Did you hear about the pointless argument between two Minecrafters?

A: They just kept going around in squares.

■

Q: Did you hear about the Minecrafter who wanted to be in the military?

A: He tried to join the Prismarines!

■

Q: Did you hear about the Wolves that were tamed by a flower patch?

A: It was puppies in poppies!

Q: Did you hear about the pirate who played *Minecraft*?
A: All he wanted to make was Planks!

■

Q: Did you hear about the Shulker movie?
A: It was a shell out!

■

Q: Did you hear the Magma Cubes got into Steve's crops?
A: It was a hot potato!

■

Q: Did you hear what happened when a Hostile Mob trampled a potato garden?
A: It was a monster mash.

■

Q: Did you hear about the wrapped gift for the Skeleton?
A: All it wanted was the bow!

■

Q: Did you hear the joke about the shelter?
A: It hasn't been made yet!

Q: Did you hear about the nervous sea monster?

A: It was a shaken Kraken!

■

Q: Did you hear they added portals to *Minecraft PE*?

A: Better late than Nether.

■

Q: Did you hear about the Minecrafter who liked playing in the nether?

A: It was lava at first sight.

■

Q: Did you hear about Alex giving Steve some Hay?

A: She really baled him out.

■

Q: Did you hear about Steve's son?

A: He's a chip off the old block.

■

Q: Did you hear about the party the Ice Gollum threw?

A: It was a snow ball.

Q: Did you hear about the Ghast dance?

A: It was a fireball!

■

Q: Did you hear about the toxic mineshaft?

A: It was rotten to the ore.

■

Q: Did you hear that Steve didn't want to have his picture taken?

A: His face was covered with Netherwarts.

■

Q: Did you hear how Steve gave Alex a Ladder when she asked for a Torch?

A: It was the wrung answer.

■

Q: Did you hear about the Mob that spawned in Ireland?

A: It was Dublin!

■

Q: Did you hear about the sad fruit crop?

A: It was so melon-choly.

Q: Did you hear the joke Steve told a Tree?

A: It had quite a punch-line.

■

Q: Did you hear the Minecrafter's story about the time he discovered a pit that went on forever?

A: There are some holes in the story.

■

Q: Did you hear the joke about *Minecraft*?

A: It's pitful.

CHAPTER 4

THE NAME GAME

A Glowstone plays *Shinecraft*.

If the 8-bit characters had one more bit, *Minecraft* would be called *Ninecraft*.

Horses play *Equinecrat*.

Ocelots play *Felinecraft*.

Wolves play *Caninecraft*.

At the Beach biome you play *Coastlinecraft*.

Witches making potions play *Combinecraft*.

In France, they play *Seinecraft*.

In Germany, they play *Rhinecraft*.

Ancient civilizations play *Mayancraft*.

The creator of *Goosebumps* plays *R.L. Stinecraft*.

Tarzan plays *Vinecraft*.

When you quit the game, you *Resigncraft*.

Q: What's the most popular sitcom in *Minecraft*?
A: *Minefeld.*

■

Q: What's a good name for a fishing pole?
A: Rod!

■

Q: What's a good name for a Shulker?
A: Shelly!

■

Q: What's a good name for a Guardian?
A: Spike!

■

Q: What's a good name for a husk?
A: Sunny!

■

Q: Why is Alex named Alex?
A: Because if she were named Steve, that would be *very* confusing.

Q: What did the Enderman name his daughter?
A: Pearl.

■

Q: What's a good name for a Creeper?
A: Boomer.

■

Q: Who is a Blaze's favorite *Pokémon* character?
A: Ash.

■

Q: What's another name for a Zombie Pigman?
A: Back bacon.

■

Q: What former president would love *Minecraft*?
A: Woodblock Wilson.

Great names for Minecraters

- Sandy
- Rocky
- Clay
- Moss
- Stone
- Brick
- Lily
- Fern
- Chester
- Roofus
- Mason

■

Q: What's a better name for a Pumpkin?
A: Jack.

■

Q: What's a good name for a Melon?
A: Melony.

■

Q: What school do *Minecraft* farmers go to?
A: Carnegie Melon.

Q: What did Steve name the first Potato he grew?
A: Chip.

Q: What actor do *Minecraft* horses love?
A: Christian Bale.

■

Q: What comedian loves *Minecraft*?
A: Chris Rock.

Q: Who's a Minecrafter's favorite actress?

A: Emma Redstone.

■

Q: What do you call three Husks?

A: The Three Husketeers!

Q: What golfer loves *Minecraft*?

A: Taiga Woods.

■

Q: What did Taiga Woods do to his plot of land?

A: He left a hole in one!

■

What does "NPC" *really* stand for?

- Not particularly consequential.
- Newly pin-cushioned.
- No point character.
- No Portal control.
- Not playing? Cool!
- New player crutch.
- Needs punching, convenient.
- Needlessly poor combatants.
- *Now* play Creative Mode.

■

Q: What's an Enderman's favorite spooky story?

A: *The Invisible Man.*

Q: What *Shark Tank* star must love *Minecraft*?
A: Mark Cube-an.

■

Q: Who is a Blaze's favorite actor?
A: Ashen Kutcher.

■

Q: What author do Witches like best?
A: Edgar Allan Poe-tion.

■

Q: What do you call *Minecraft* Steve when he's not building anything?
A: Steve!

■

Q: What do you call a Ghast named Lee?
A: Ghast-lee.

■

Q: What do you call a Minecrafter who loves using the Swords most of all?
A: Lance.

Q: What did the Blaze name its daughter?

A: Ashley.

Q: Where does Steve buy his building supplies?

A: Wall-Mart.

Q: What social network does Steve use?

A: Faceblock.

Q: Who's an important Creeper pioneer?

A: Daniel Boom!

CHAPTER 5

THAT'S ENTERTAINMENT!

Minecraft Movies

Holes

The Village

Gleaming the Cube

Jungle 2 Jungle

Spawn

Creepshow

Here Comes the Boom

Shaft

Elder Guardians of the Galaxy

The Ghast House on the Left

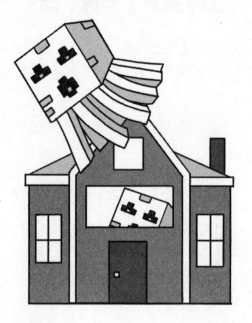

Mojangle All the Way

Clean Slate

Enderman's Game

Pixels

Married to the Mob

Field of Dreams

Romancing the Stone

The Jewel of the Nile

Frankenstone

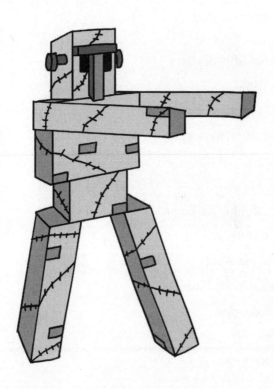

In Like Flint

Fences

Jonah Vex

Iron Ore Man

Diamonds are Forever

Songs for Minecrafters

"Let it Blow"

"Gold Digger"

"Everybody Clays the Fool"

"All I Axe"

"I, Me, Mine"

"Like a Rolling Redstone"

"Let's Get Rocked"

"Dust in the Wind"

"Pickaxe Up the Pieces"

"Mr. Mojangles"

"Notcho Man"

"Just One Persson"

"Always on My Mine"

"Holding Out for a Herobrine"

"TNT"

"Man in the Box"

"Dynomite"

"This is The End"

"It's the End of the World as We Know It (And I Feel Fine)"

"Until The End"

"Coal Me Maybe"

"We Built This City"

"Welcome to the Jungle"

"I Wanna Rock"

"Hard Rock Life"

"Rock On"

"Rock'n Me"

"Big Rock Candy Mountain"

"We Will Rock You"

"Down on the Corner"

"Build Me Up, Buttercup"

"Another Brick in the Wall"

"Loves Me Like a Rock"

"Brick House"

"Like a Rock"

"I'm Not Your Stepping Stone"

"Solid as a Rock"

"Shine On You Crazy Diamond"

"You Dropped a Bomb on Me"

"The Boxer"

"Rock Lobster"

"Rock Around the Clock"

"Rocks-Anne"

"It's All In the Game"

"Monster Mash"

"How Deep Is Your Mine?"

"How to Save a Game"

"Light My Fire"

"Fallin'"

"Rock With You"

"Creep"

"Ain't No Mountain High Enough"

"Drop It Like It's Hot"

"Change the World"

"Blaze Of Glory"

"Heart Of Gold"

"Rock Me Gently"

"You've Got the Torch"

"Don't Let The Sun Go Down On Me

"Rockstar"

"Rock On"

"If I Had A Hammer"

"Hungry Like the Wolf"

"I Am a Rock"

"Roam"

"Here Comes the Rain Again"

"What Does the Rocks Say?"

"This Old Cart of Mine"

"U Can't Torch This"

"Building a Mystery"

"Stayin' Alive"

Minecraft Musicians

The Rolling Redstones

Neil Diamond

M. C. Hammer

Ice-TNT

Pebbles

John Melon-block

Ed Shearin'

Minecraft TV

House

Torch, Wood

The Gold Ore Girls

Ore-tlandia

Steve Universe

SpongeBrick CubePants

King of the Extreme Hills

The Ghast Man on Earth

iZombie Pigman

8 Bits is Enough

Square Pegs

The Flintstones

Chopped

This is Cac-tus

Bob the Builder

Books for Minecrafters

The Giving Tree

Chick Chicka Boom Boom

Oh, the Biomes You'll Go!

Little House on the Prairie

Sylvester and the Magic Pebble

Where the Red Stone Grows

Where the Redstone Glows

Minecraft Board Games

Chest

Carts Against Humanity

Ore-peration

S-ore-y

Pick-tionary

Bat-Gammon

Axes and Allies

The Amazing Superhero . . . The Incredible Steve!

He can . . .

- Break trees with a feather!
- Chop logs with his hands!
- Carry a mountain in his pocket!
- Make white wool red!
- Shear sheep with just his hands!
- Fuse things together with his hands!
- Jump off mountains and survive!
- Never break a bone!
- Discover huge stores of diamonds and emeralds!

Minecraft Sports Teams

Chicago Polar Bears

Cincinnati Redstones

Washington Redstones

Pittsburgh Steelers

Denver Gold Nuggets

Baltimore Ore-ioles

Ore-izona Diamondbacks

Dallas Cow-Boys

Portland Trail-Blazes

Minnesota Timber-Wolves

Detroit Pistons

Arizona Diamondbacks

Colorado Rockies

Los Angeles Shearers

Phoenix Sunstones

Washington Witches

Toronto Leaves

St. Louis Lapiz Lazuli

Other Video Games for Minecrafters

Double Ender Dragon

Diamond Gear Solid

Grand Theft Minecart

Elder Guardian Scrolls

BiomeShock

Q: Why can't you score against Minecrafters who play basketball?

A: They know how to block.

■

Q: Who's the most popular wrestler in *Minecraft*?

A: The Rock.

■

Q: What's a Blaze's favorite hockey team?

A: The Calgary Flames.

■

Q: Why can't Silverfish play basketball?

A: Because they always stay away from the net.

■

Q: What did Charlie Brown say when Steve broke his baseball bat?

A: "You Blockhead!"

Q: What sport does Steve do for fun?

A: Rock climbing.

Q: How is the Nether like a baseball game?

A: The Bats.

Q: Why do Minecrafters like tennis?
A: Because it's played on quartz.

■

Q: What band is popular in the snowy Biomes?
A: Coldplay.

■

Q: What's a Minecrafter's favorite cable TV station?
A: TNT.

■

Q: What's a Minecrafter's favorite *Lord of the Rings* character?
A: Golem.

■

Q: What kind of music do Iron Golems play?
A: Heavy Metal!

■

Q: What compositions are Steve's favorites?
A: Bach's.

Q: What three composers do Chickens like best?
A: Bach, Bach, Bach!

■

Q: What do Rabbits listen to?
A: Hip hop.

■

Q: What band is most popular in the Villages?
A: The Village People.

■

Q: What radio station do Minecrafters listen to?
A: The golden oldies station.

■

Q: How do you know Skeleton mobs are approaching?
A: You can hear the trom-bones.

■

Q: What song do Zombies hate?
A: "You Are My Sunshine."

CHAPTER 6

YOU KNOW YOU'RE A MINECRAFTER IF . . .

Your dream job? Digging ditches.

You call something "the pits," and mean it as a compliment.

You go to rock shops and are disappointed by how small everything is.

A real-life chest full of diamonds would excite you less than one in *Minecraft*.

You've hurt your hands getting firewood.

You wish dirt floated in real life.

You know that the best protection is a door.

You sleep with the lights on . . . to stop mobs from spawning.

You pass a construction site and wonder why it's taking them so long to finish.

You've considered taming a wolf by giving it a bone.

There's a coal mine in your backyard.

You're frustrated that it takes years for trees to grow in your yard.

You cut all your food into cubes.

You're a professional griefer.

You learned Swedish to better keep aware of update rumors.

You wish your watch could just tell you when dawn and dusk happen.

The idea of finding gold in real life doesn't thrill you.

When dusk falls, you panic and run home.

You've planted cacti, just to be safe.

You carry a bunch of tools everywhere you go..

You think horse racing would be a lot more interesting if the jockeys rode spiders instead.

All you eat is bacon.

Your go-to meal: two-mushroom stew.

Anytime you find gravel, you sift through it looking for flint.

You've put sand in the oven to try to turn it into glass.

Your trips to famous buildings don't thrill you because you made the same ones in *Minecraft*.

Your front door has a pressure plate.

You dream in pixels.

All your buckets got burned with lava.

Minesweeper disappoints you.

CHAPTER 7
SWIFTLY, ALEX!

"Look at my shiny new structure!" said Alex, waxing enthusiastic.

"The Ocelot is stuck on the roof and is not happy about it," said Alex uproariously.

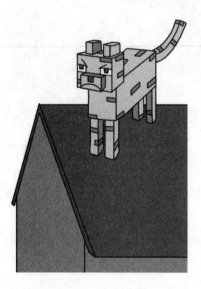

"That's a very large Guardian," said Alex superficially.

"Looks like it's about to rain again," said Alex precipitously.

"I'm not afraid of Ocelots," Alex whimpurred.

"Stay out of my Gold mine!" Alex claimed.

"That's a lovely mirror!" said Alex reflectively.

"That Husk is falling apart since the last time I saw it," said Alex neurotically.

"This meat sure is hard to chew," Alex beefed jerkily.

"I just punched a bunch of Trees," said Alex lumberingly.

"Of course I can make armor," Alex replied by mail.

"I'm taking this boat back to the dock," Alex reported.

"I'm meeting Steve at the Beach tonight," said Alex sedately.

"I've lost quite a few as well," said Alex winsomely.

"I don't like sweet potatoes," Alex yammered.

"Let's put down some tracks," Alex railed.

"Rowing this boat makes my hands hurt," said Alex callously.

"All my Torches went out!" said Alex delightedly.

"There's nothing here but sand," said Alex grittily.

"This Redstone weighs a ton," said Alex heavily.

"I left the door ajar," said Alex openly.

"I wish I hadn't built this winding staircase," said Alex coyly.

"This Chest is empty!" Alex hollered.

"Someone stole all my Glass blocks," said Alex painlessly.

"My garden needs another layer of Moss," Alex repeated.

"That shelter build was baaaaaad," bleated Alex sheepishly.

"Oops, I've ripped my pants!" was Alex's unseemly comment.

"The roof is about to collapse," Alex upheld.

CHAPTER 8

RHYME TIME

Q: If a green hostile played soccer, it would be at this position.

A: Creeper Keeper.

Q: A certain green Hostile keeps its school assignments in here.

A: A Trapper Creeper.

Q: How does a Mob get in a house?

A: With the Mob knob.

Q: How do you disarm a Mob?

A: Rob the mob.

Q: What's the difference between a Ghast and a Chicken?

A: One's in the Nether and the other drops a feather.

Q: What does Steve do when he goes out the door?

A: Steve leaves.

Q: How does Steve throw a heavy block?

A: Steve heaves.

■

Q: How does Steve turn Wool into a blanket?

A: Steve weaves.

■

Q: Where does Steve keep his arms?

A: In Steve's sleeves.

■

Q: What does Steve do when the Creepers blow up his house and all his Sheep?

A: Steve grieves.

■

Q: Why is Steve such a good builder?

A: Because Steve achieves!

■

Q: What would you call hardcore Alex fans?

A: Alex fanatics.

Q: What would you find in a nearly-empty Nether?
A: The last Ghast.

◼

Q: What's the hottest puzzle in *Minecraft*?
A: A Blaze maze.

◼

Q: What kind of cowhide should you wear in the underworld?
A: Nether Leather.

◼

Q: What's another name for a *Minecraft* coding mistake?
A: A Notch botch.

◼

Q: How does the creator of *Minecraft* tell time?
A: With Notch's watch.

Q: What do you call a spell-casting Hostile who has a ton of potions?

A: A rich Witch.

ALEX: Steve, what do Iron Ingots and Steel have in common?

STEVE: They're both metallics, Alex!

■

Q: What should you look out for when exploring caves in *Minecraft*?

A: If there's a Spider inside there.

■

Q: What does Alex say when she wants to be alone?

A: "Leave, Steve!"

■

Q: What's the slowest thing in The End?

A: A draggin' Dragon.

■

Q: Who cleans up the mess after those bad green guys blow up?

A: The Creeper Sweeper.

Q: **What did Steve call his trip to the biome of Grass, Vines, Lily Pads, and Slime?**

A: A Swamp romp.

■

Q: **What did Alex do when she needed to build a house?**

A: She went on a Birch search.

■

Q: **What do you call a Hostile who cries a lot?**

A: A Creeper Weeper.

■

Q: **Why was Steve happy to see Alex in the final dimension of *Minecraft*?**

A: Because it's good to have a friend in The End.

■

Q: **Did you hear about how Steve went on and on and on about his favorite caverns?**

A: Yeah, it was a real Cave Rave.

Q: What's another name for a Jockey?
A: A Spider rider.

Q: What sport do Spider riders love to play?
A: Jockey hockey.

■

Q: Why couldn't the Skeleton hit anything with its arrows?
A: Its bow was too slow.

Q: How was Steve surprised by a Creeper?

A: He must've missed the hiss.

■

Q: What's a better name for a Mob of Cows?

A: A moo crew.

■

Q: Who's made of iron and is very quiet and serious?

A: A solemn Golem.

■

Q: What do you call bad deeds in the Swamp biome?

A: Slime crime.

■

Q: In what kind of house would you find a good digging tool?

A: A Shovel hovel.

■

Q: What kind of pots does Alex like in her houses?

A: Alex? Ceramics.

Q: What do Mobs eat?

A: Hostile pasta.

■

Q: What kind of drink do experienced builders drink?

A: Silk milk.

■

Q: What do you call the wind in *Minecraft*?

A: A *Minecraft* Draft.

■

Q: What do you call a thief who picks through an explosion?

A: A rubble robber.

■

Q: How are sports different in *Minecraft*?

A: There's no score—just Ore.

Creepers are green,

Cave Spiders are black,

Sorry—it looks like your shelter is under attack!

■

Roses are red, violets are blue.

If you're gonna play *Minecraft*

The Creeper will creep you!

CHAPTER 9

TONGUE TWISTERS

Crooked crafters crumble quickly.

Big bad blocks block big blocky boulders.

Pick a pack of puny Pickaxes.

Silly Steve switched skins on Sunday.

Billy built blocks bit by bit.

Skating Squids squawk silly songs.

Wooly Wolves wash wobbly Watermelons.

Steve smelt six slinky silver Swords.

Dropped leather, chicken feather.

Short swords.

Sick sick shorn Sheep.

Don't ask a Pickaxe when you can pick a Pickaxe.

Don't be the last to be aghast at a Ghast.

Build a big brick building!

Notch knows not what?

Practical Cactus.

The Enderman might mind, but the Endermite might not mind.

The last Ghast passed fast.

Witches potions, riches in oceans.

Which Witch mob mobbed you?

Blazes bounce blocks by the Beach biome.

Rob the Mob before the Mob robs Bob!

Sneaky Slimes slowly slide.

Spooky Spiders slither hither.

Torches light the night quite brightly.

Guardians guard and Golems get going, got it?

Shulky shells seems shady.

A Vex wrecked Alex, but Alex hexed the Vex.

Shush, Husk, shush!

The Shulker sulked in its purple Purpur.

Red mushroom, brown mushroom.

Only Ocelots own own oily Ores.

Purpurs, parrots, and pearls, please!

Guardians and Ghasts and a go-go!

A Wither left a Leather Lever in the Nether.

Can't the color of Coal ore be a cooler color?

A quart of Quartz or a quarter of quartz ore?

Whether the Wither be fine
Or whether the Wither be not.
Whether the Wither be cold
Or whether the Wither be hot.
We'll weather the Wither
Whatever the Wither
Whether we like it or not.

Minecraft Mix-Em-Ups

The first letters of each word have been flipped with the first letters of the second word. Can you decode these mixed-up Minecraft *words?*

Skither Weleton

Rishing Fod

Owe and Barrows

Hextreme Ills

Bone Steach

Pombie Zigman

Lest Choot

Nold Gugget

Go Snolem

Wame Tolf

Runny Babbit

Hog Louse

Bay Hales

Chork Pop

Stedrone

Block of Flats

Pass grath

Birt dlock

Answers:

Wither Skeleton

Fishing Rod

Bow and Arrows

Extreme Ills

Stone Beach

Zombie Pigman

Chest Loot

Gold Nugget

Snow Golem

Tame Wolf

Bunny Rabbit

Log House

Hay Bales

Pork Chop

Redstone

Flock of Bats

Grass Path

Dirt Block

CHAPTER 10
JUST PLAIN SILLY

Q: Did you hear about the *Minecraft* material that wanted to be a singer?

A: It worked the Redstone Circuit.

■

Q: But did you ever actually hear it sing?

A: It was positively electric!

■

Q: What's the difference between *Minecraft* when it started, and today?

A: Back then it was just one Persson.

■

Q: How did Steve walk after he broke his leg in a mineshaft?

A: He used a Sugarcane.

Q: What's a Skeleton's favorite TV show?
A: *Bones*.

■

Q: Are Skeletons the most fearsome of all the mobs?
A: Sure—there are no bones about it!

■

Q: Where would you find the Nether?
A: On a Netherrack.

■

Q: In *Minecraft*, what's the land that's the farthest away?
A: The Far Lands!

■

Q: Where do Skeletons hate to watch videos?
A: On Vine—they can't see anything!

■

Q: Where do *Minecraft* Cows watch videos?
A: On Bo-Vine.

Q: Why did Steve put on his blue shirt and blue pants?

A: He was feeling very blue.

■

Q: Why do cats love *Minecraft*?

A: Because it's a sandbox game.

■

Q: Did you hear about the Minecrafter who got disappointed watching the Kentucky Derby?

A: She was hoping to see a Chicken Jockey.

■

Q: Which creature in Minecraft has the raspiest voice?

A: The Horses!

■

Q: What's more valuable than a Diamond in Minecraft?

A: *Two* Diamonds in Minecraft.

Q: Did you hear about the not-very-smart Minecrafter?

A: He thought he was going to get in trouble for making stained glass.

■

Q: What kind of pie do Minecrafters eat?

A: Cobblerstone.

■

Q: What kind of *Minecraft* is simple but delicious?

A: Vanilla *Minecraft*.

■

Q: Did you hear what happened when some lava fell in a Minecart?

A: It combined to form the Magma arta!

■

Q: What's the difference between a metal work tool and a Creeper?

A: One's an Anvil, and one's an evil.

Q: Who brings toys to all the good boys and girls who
    live in the Ocean biome?

A: Sandy Claus.

Q: What material did Steve look for when he needed to clean his house?

A: Sponge!

■

Q: What's a good name for a Snow Golem?

A: Gourd.

■

Q: What material would you get a Minecrafter on their birthday?

A: Cake!

■

Q: What did the Magma Cube say when it saw another Magma Cube?

A: "I think I'm in lava!"

■

Q: Why did Steve lose his shovel?

A: Because a Creeper blew up his house.

Q: What's green and has wheels?

A: A Creeper. I was just kidding about the wheels.

■

Q: What's the smelliest ore in *Minecraft*?

A: You can smell the things in *Minecraft*?! That's amazing!

■

Q: What did the Creeper say to the other Creeper?

A: "You're creepin' me out!"

■

Q: What did one Skeleton say to the other Skeleton?

A: "Hello!"

■

A Creeper walked into a room . . . and everybody got out of there *fast*.

■

Q: What's the hardest thing in *Minecraft*?

A: *Minecraft* on hard mode.

Q: **What's a Creeper's favorite color?**
A: Blew.

■

Q: **What's a beginning Minecrafter's favorite kind of music?**
A: Bedrock.

■

Q: **Did you hear about the not-very-smart Minecrafter who got covered in painful spikes?**
A: There was a cactus outside his house and when he realized that it wasn't a Creeper, he gave it a hug.

■

Q: **Did you hear the one about Redstone delay?**
A: Never mind, I'd just be repeating.

■

Q: **Did you hear about the *Minecraft* Dog that joined Twitter?**
A: He just really liked to follow people.

Q: How did Steve get an ache in his arm?

A: He had a glitch he was trying to scratch.

■

Q: Did you hear about the *Minecraft* joke fan?

A: What a square!

■

Q: What's the dirtiest block in *Minecraft*?

A: Dirt!

■

Q: What did Alex say when Steve asked for an Air Block?

A: "Air you go!"

■

Q: Did you hear about the Redstone that was knighted?

A: It insisted that everybody call it Sir-Cuit.

■

Q: What happened when the not-very-smart Minecrafter put ice cream into a furnace?

A: It smelted.

Q: What's a Minecrafter's favorite kind of fish?
A: Smelt.

■

Steve: What are you looking for?

Alex: Ore.

Steve: Or what?

Alex: No, ore.

Steve: There's no Ore?! Oh no! Let's go look for some more!

■

Q: Why did the Creeper jump into a lake?
A: It wanted to take a sssssssshower.

■

Q: How does Steve stay so strong?
A: He lifts Iron.

■

Q: What phone company does Steve use?
A: Sprint.

Q: What's an Ender Dragon's favorite part of a movie?
A: The End.

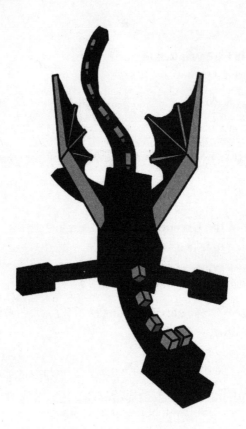

Q: How does Steve keep his shirts wrinkle-free?
A: In *Minecraft*, Irons are everywhere!

■

Q: Why is a Squid so good in battle?
A: Because they're well-armed.

■

Steve: Where did you get that armor?

Alex: You like it?

Steve: Yes, do you have any for me?

Alex: Armor in the closet!

■

Q: What's the best kind of Ocelot?
A: An ace-lot!

■

Q: What's the difference between a *Minecraft* cat and a treasure trove of Diamonds?
A: One's an Ocelot, and one's an awesome lot!

Q: How did Steve prevent Mobs from getting into his house?

A: He blocked the doors.

Q: What did the Tree say to Steve when he kept punching it for Wood?

A: "Hey, leaf me alone!"

Q: Why did Notch finally add Pistons to the game?

A: He was tired of people pushing him.

Q: Why are Minecrafters such good swordfighters?

A: They have lots of practice with fencing!

Q: Why are Minecrafters so good at tongue twisters?

A: They love s-wordplay.

Q: What do Australian Creepers use to take down their enemies?

A: BOOM-a-rangs.

■

Q: Did you hear about the mob of Skeletons who got hungry and went to the Village?

A: They ordered spare ribs.

■

Q: What's a Creeper's favorite food?

A: Ssssssssalad.

■

Q: Why do they like it so much?

A: Because it's green.

■

Q: How come poison ivy isn't a plant you'll find in *Minecraft*?

A: Because if the Witches came across it, you'd wind up with some itchy witchies!

Q: Did you hear about the breakdancing Creeper?

A: It could really "pop" and "block."

■

Q: What did the Chicken say to the Sheep?

A: "It's nice to meet ewe."

Q: In what city would you find a *Minecraft* wolf?
A: Howllywood!

∎

Q: Why aren't there any cars in *Minecraft*?
A: What would be the point? The streets are always blocked.

∎

Q: Why couldn't the Minecrafter join the military or vote?
A: Because he was a miner.

∎

Q: What did the Sheep say after trying to eat a cactus?
A: "I didn't see the point."

∎

Q: With all that time outside, how come Steve and Alex never get sunburned?
A: They use plenty of sun-block.

Q: Did you hear *Minecraft* has turkeys now?

A: Listen closely and you'll hear them say "cobble, cobble, cobble."

■

Q: Did you hear about the Skeleton that went to a U2 concert?

A: It desperately wanted to meet Bone-O.

■

Q: What do Minecrafters do when they want to go out and have fun?

A: They go to square dances.

■

Q: Why couldn't the miner ever find the stash of Diamonds buried near her favorite digging spot?

A: There was always something blocking her way.

■

Q: Did you hear about the not-very-smart Minecrafter who needed a dozen eggs?

A: Yeah, he just bought six eggs and then waited for them to spawn.

Q: Which is the oldest Mob in *Minecraft*?
A: The Elder Guardian.

■

Q: Which Mob do trees in *Minecraft* like best?
A: The Alder Guardian.

■

Q: What *Minecraft* Mob is made completely of metal?
A: The Welder Guardian.

■

Q: What's the difference between a tamable Mob and an Ocelot?
A: One's a Mule, and the other mewls.

■

Q: Why is it so hard to find corn in *Minecraft*?
A: Because it's always hiding behind the Husks.

■

Q: What's the difference between a *Minecraft* structure and a white-furred Mob?
A: One is the bearer of poles, and other is a polar bear.

Knock-knock!

Who's there?

Vera.

Vera who?

Vera few people think Herobrine is real.

■

Knock-knock!

Who's there?

Luke.

Luke who?

Luke before you dig!

■

Knock-knock!

Who's there?

Wayne.

Wayne who?

The Wayne is coming down, so it's a great time to go fishing!

■

Knock-knock!

Who's there?

Betty.

Betty who?

It's Betty-bye time for your house when there's a Creeper around.

■

Knock-knock!

Who's there?

Noah.

Noah who?

Noah any good places to find Prismarine?

■

Knock-knock!

Who's there?

Diana.

Diana who?

Diana-mals are everywhere in *Minecraft*!

■

Knock-knock!

Who's there?

Bowen.

Bowen who?

Bowen arrow is what a skeleton carries.

∎

Knock-knock!

Who's there?

Harvey.

Harvey who?

Harvey having fun yet playing *Minecraft*?

∎

Knock-knock!

Who's there?

Leslie.

Leslie who?

Leslie on a Fence and see if we can make it fall over!

∎

Knock-knock!

Who's there?

Emerson.

Emerson who?

Emerson nice Emeralds you've got there.

■

Knock-knock!

Who's there?

Kara.

Kara who?

Kara to share some of those Emeralds you've got there?

■

Knock-knock!

Who's there?

Gladys.

Gladys who?

Gladys you . . . and not a Creeper!

■

Knock-knock!

Who's there?

Renée.

Renée who?

Renée really fast from some Witches today!

Knock-knock!

Who's there?

Philip.

Philip who?

Philip a bucket with water!

■

Knock-knock!

Who's there?

Hannah.

Hannah who?

Hannah me my tools and let's go mining!

■

Knock-knock!

Who's there?

Dig.

Dig who?

Dig? Me? You? Right now? Let's go!

■

Knock-knock!

Who's there?

Maya.

Maya who?

Maya hand is killing me from punching trees.

■

Knock-knock!

Who's there?

Enid.

Enid who?

If Enid anything, I'll be mining.

■

Knock-knock!

Who's there?

Joanna.

Joanna who?

Joanna tell me where you got those Diamonds?

■

Knock-knock!

Who's there?

Barbara.

Barbara who?

Barbara is what a Sheep says.

■

Knock-knock!

Who's there?

Stan.

Stan who?

Stan back, I'm going to use some TNT!

■

Knock-knock!

Who's there?

Denise.

Denise who?

Denise is where a skeleton shoots you.

■

Knock-knock!

Who's there?

Lydia.

Lydia who?

Lydia chest looks a bit loose. Better fix it or all of your items will fall out!

■

Knock-knock!

Who's there?

Emma.

Emma who?

Emma bit low on materials. Can I borrow some from you?

■

Knock-knock!

Who's there?

Wilma.

Wilma who?

Wilma house stay standing after a Creeper comes to visit?

■

Knock-knock

Who's there?

Althea.

Althea who?

Althea later, I'm going mining!

■

Knock-knock!

Who's there?

Daisy.

Daisy who?

Daisy good time to play *Minecraft*.

■

Knock-knock!

Who's there?

Good night.

Good night who?

Good night? Never, because that's when the Mobs come out!

■

Knock-knock!

Who's there?

Rhoda.

Rhoda who?

Rhoda Boat in the water today!

■

Knock-knock!

Who's there?

Ron.

Ron who?

Ron really fast until you're sprinting!

■

Knock-knock

Who's there?

Oliver.

Oliver who?

Be careful, or Oliver stuff is going to get blown up by Griefers!

■

Knock-knock!

Who's there?

Harriet.

Harriet who?

Harriet a green Potato. It was so gross!

■

Knock-knock!

Who's there?

Annette.

Annette who?

Annette from you and my expertise, and we're sure to catch some fish in no time!

■

Q: What did Steve's dog do when he gave it some food?
A: He "wolfed" it down!

■

Q: What does Steve do when he gets frustrated after a day of fruitless mining?
A: He cools off by taking a walk around the block.

Q: Why don't Minecrafters read *Peanuts*?
A: They don't like how Lucy uses "blockhead" as an insult!

■

Q: Did you hear that Steve got a brand new set of tools?
A: They were in Flint condition!

■

Q: What's smaller than the smallest Magma Cubes?
A: Tiny Magma Cubes!

■

Q: What's a Skeleton's favorite flower?
A: Yarrow!

■

Q: Why did the Polar Bear leave Steve alone?
A: It wanted to remain Neutral.

■

Q: Did you hear about the huge group of Witches that threw potions at Steve?
A: Talk about a mob of Mob lobbers!

Q: What's the difference between Glass and an important *Minecraft* cutting tool?

A: One is sheer, and the other is Shears.

■

Q: What do the sky in *Minecraft* and a roller coaster have in common?

A: They've both got height restrictions.

■

A Spider couldn't keep his balance on the ice. The other Spider said to him, "Slick move!"

■

Q: How did the Vindicator feel after a good attack?

A: Vindicated!

■

Steve: Do you need these pieces of Wood to make a boat?

Alex: I do. Planks!

Steve: Yes, that's what they are. Do you need them to build a Boat or not?

Q: **Why was the bow so good at taking down Hostile Mobs in the morning?**
A: It was just feeling charged!

■

Q: **What part of buffets do Minecrafters like?**
A: The hot bar.

■

Q: **What's a Minecrafter's favorite prehistoric creature?**
A: A wool-y mammoth.

■

Q: **How do you heal wounds in a dungeon?**
A: Dungeon unguent.

■

Q: **Why did Steve throw a jukebox in a furnace?**
A: He wanted to hear some hot tunes!

■

Q: **What part of *Minecraft* has the most trees?**
A: Oak-lahoma.

Steve had a big plan to build big rocks out of tiny rocks. But then it seemed like a whole lot of pointless work, and from there, his plans un-graveled.

■

Q: What happens when Spiders in *Minecraft* find corn?
A: They make cob-webs!

■

Did you hear that a bunch of Witches got together to throw potions at Steve and then eat birthday take? It was a real Splash Bash!

■

Q: What's the difference between a programming error in Minecraft and a Hostile that throws potions?
A: One's a glitch, and the other's a Witch!

■

Steve will always remember the first time he ever built his own crafting station. Building that workbench was a true bench-mark moment.

Q: Why didn't the Creeper have any friends?

A: Because he was such a Creep!

■

Q: What's "Steve" short for, anyway?

A: Steven!

■

Did you hear about the irate Creeper? He was always losing his head about something.

Q: **What's the difference between a Chest full of diamonds and a Hut?**

A: One's full of riches, while the other is full of Witches!

■

Q: **What's the best way to see what the Nether is really like?**

A: Just watch the Nether Channel.

CHAPTER 11

THIS IS THE END

Q: Where's the best place to spot an Enderman?
A: Right next to you, all of a sudden!

■

Q: What did one Enderman say to the other Enderman?
A: "You're outta sight!"

■

Q: What happens when you cross an Enderman with a Ghast?
A: Pearly whites!

■

Q: Why did the Enderman not stick around?
A: He had teleportant business!

Q: Where do Endermen keep their stuff?

A: Ender chest.

Q: What do you call an Enderman when it just spawned?

A: An Enderboy.

Q: Why would an Enderman make a good police officer?

A: Because they could be the long arm of the law!

Q: Why do they call them Endermites?
A: Tread lightly Endermite leave you and your stuff alone!

■

Q: Why did the Enderman turn down a new job?
A: He just couldn't see himself doing it.

■

Q: Why is The End so troublesome?
A: Because it's got a bad altitude.

■

Q: What did the Endermen say to the miners?
A: "Respect your enders!"

■

Q: What will you never find in an Enderman's house?
A: Stairs!

■

Q: What's at the back of the Enderman's house?
A: The End!

Q: What happened when the Enderman went to the doctor?

A: The doctor said, "I'm sorry, but I can't see you right now."

■

Q: Why can't the Ender Dragon ever understand a book?

A: Because it always starts at The End!

■

Q: Why did the Enderman leave the party?

A: Because everyone was staring at him.

■

Q: Why did the Enderman cross the road?

A: He didn't. He teleported!

■

Q: What will Endermen do to you?

A: Scare you out of your mine!

Q: **What's as big as an Ender Dragon but doesn't weigh anything?**

A: An Ender Dragon's shadow.

Q: **What happens when you cross a Creeper with an Enderman?**

A: A teleporting bomb.

Q: What do you get when you cross a car with a neutral humanoid mob?

A: A Fenderman.

■

Q: What do you call a skinny resident of The End?

A: A Slenderman.

■

Q: What mob is good at gymnastics?

A: Bendermen.

Q: What resident of The End wastes all their money?
A: A Spenderman.

■

Q: What resident of The End will loan you all their money?
A: A Lenderman.

■

Q: Where do Endermen go when they teleport?
A: Teleportland.

■

Q: What part of a house is most like an Enderman?
A: The stair-well.

■

Q: What's at the end of The End?
A: The letter "D"!

■

Q: What did Steve say when he wandered into The End?
A: "Well, it looks like this is The End."

Q: What did Steve say when he was cornered by an Ender Dragon?

A: "I guess this really is The End!"